Felix Mendelssohn

COMPLETE CHAMBER MUSIC FOR STRINGS

Edited by Julius Rietz

From the Breitkopf & Härtel Complete Works Edition

Dover Publications, Inc.
New York

Published in Canada by General Publishing Company, Ltd., 30 Lesmill Road, Don Mills, Toronto, Ontario.
Published in the United Kingdom by Constable and Company, Ltd., 10 Orange Street, London WC2H 7EG.

This Dover edition, first published in 1978, is an unabridged republication of the following two complete series from *Felix Mendelssohn Bartholdy's Werke. Kritisch durchgesehene Ausgabe von Julius Rietz. Mit Genehmigung der Originalverleger* (complete edition published between 1874 and 1877):

Serie 5. Kammermusik für fünf und mehrere Saiteninstrumente.

Serie 6. Quartette für 2 Violinen Bratsche und Violoncell.

International Standard Book Number: 0-486-23679-X
Library of Congress Catalog Card Number: 78-54971

Manufactured in the United States of America
Dover Publications, Inc.
180 Varick Street
New York, N.Y. 10014

CONTENTS

	page
Octet in E-flat Major, Op. 20, for 4 Violins, 2 Violas and 2 Violoncelli (composed 1825; dedicated to Eduard Rietz; first published by Breitkopf & Härtel, Leipzig)	
Allegro moderato ma con fuoco	1
Andante	16
Scherzo. Allegro leggierissimo	23
Presto	33
Quintet No. 1 in A Major, Op. 18, for 2 Violins, 2 Violas and Violoncello (composed 1826 & 1832; first published by N. Simrock, Berlin)	
Allegro con moto	49
Intermezzo. Andante sostenuto	60
Scherzo. Allegro di molto	66
Allegro vivace	75
Quintet No. 2 in B-flat Major, Op. 87, for 2 Violins, 2 Violas and Violoncello (composed 1845; first published by Breitkopf & Härtel, Leipzig)	
Allegro vivace	85
Andante scherzando	97
Adagio e lento	101
Allegro molto vivace	106
Quartet No. 1 in E-flat Major, Op. 12 (composed 1829; first published by F. Hofmeister, Leipzig)	
Adagio non troppo—Allegro non tardante	114
Canzonetta. Allegretto	120
Molto allegro e vivace	124
Quartet No. 2 in A Major, Op. 13 (composed 1827; first published by Breitkopf & Härtel, Leipzig)	
Thema	134
Adagio–Allegro vivace	135
Adagio non lento	142
Intermezzo [various tempi]	146
Quartet No. 3 in D Major, Op. 44, No. 1 (composed 1838; dedicated to the Crown Prince of Sweden; first published by Breitkopf & Härtel, Leipzig)	
Molto Allegro vivace	158
Menuetto. Un poco Allegretto	167
Presto con brio	174

Quartet No. 4 in E Minor, Op. 44, No. 2 (composed 1837; dedicated to the Crown Prince of Sweden; first published by Breitkopf & Härtel, Leipzig)
Allegro assai appas[s]ionato 184
Scherzo. Allegro di molto 193
Andante 198
Presto agitato 202

Quartet No. 5 in E-flat Major, Op. 44, No. 3 (composed 1838; dedicated to the Crown Prince of Sweden; first published by Breitkopf & Härtel, Leipzig)
Allegro vivace 212
Scherzo. Assai leggiero vivace 222
Adagio non troppo 228
Molto Allegro con fuoco 232

Quartet No. 6 in F Minor, Op. 80 (composed 1847; first published by Breitkopf & Härtel, Leipzig)
Allegro vivace assai 242
Allegro assai 249
Adagio 253
Finale. Allegro molto 256

Four Pieces for String Quartet, Op. 81 (first published by Breitkopf & Härtel, Leipzig)
Andante sostenuto. Tema con variazioni (E Major; composed 1847) 264
Scherzo. Allegro leggiero (A Minor; composed 1847) 269
Capriccio. Andante con moto—Allegro fugato, assai vivace (E Minor; composed 1843) 274
Fuga. A tempo ordinario 281

Octet in E-flat Major, Op. 20

cresc.
al

dim.
p
cresc.
f
mf
sf
fp

dim.
pp
cresc.
p
f
ff
sf
fpp
sf pp
stacc.
pizz.

stacc.
stacc.
pp
stacc.
pizz.
arco
pizz.
pizz.
pizz.
arco
tr
pp
mf
cre - scen - do
cresc.
arco
cresc.

arco
arco
arco
sempre ff
con fuoco
cresc.

1.
2.

sf
ff

dim.
mf
p
f
pp con espress.
espress.
sfp
pp

cresc.
p
mf
f
ff

sempre ff
cresc.
cantabile

con espress.
poco rit.
cresc.
f
sf
fp
pp
dim.
a tempo.
stacc.
pizz.
arco

cre - - scen - - - - do
cresc.
cresc.
cresc.
cresc.
arco
cresc.
con fuoco
arco
pcresc.
con fuoco
con fuoco

cresc.

p con fuoco
cresc.
espress.
tr
ff
fp
sf

Andante.
cresc.
pizz.

dim.
pizz.
arco
sempre pp

cresc.
f
ff
dim.
p
pp
pp espress.

pp
pp
pp
pp
pp
pp
pp
pp
dolce
pp
pp
pp
pp
pp
pp
dolce
cresc.
cresc.
cresc.
cresc.
cresc.
cresc.
cresc.
cresc.
cresc.
cresc.
cresc.
cresc.
cresc.
cresc.
cresc.
cresc.
cresc.
cresc.
cresc.

cresc.
f
p
pizz.
arco

dim.
pp
espress.

dim.
pp
sul C.
dol.
espress.

Si deve suonare questo
Scherzo sempre pp e staccato.

Scherzo.

Allegro leggierissimo.

stacc.
p sf
sf
p
pp

1.
2.
pp
pizz.
p

stacc.
pizz.
arco
tr

p leggiero
dim.
pp

espress.
pizz.
arco
pp
tr
pizz.
arco
p
espress.

pp
pp stacc.
pp leggiero
tr

pp
pp
pp
pp
pp
pp
pp
pp
dim.
dim.
dim.
dim.
dim.
dim.
dim.
dim.

Presto.
f
ff

ff
p
fp
cresc.
mf
f

p
dim.
p
espress.
espress.

cresc.
espress.

cresc.
stacc.
pizz.
arco

sempre stacc.
cresc.
arco
pp
f

f
ff
sempre f

f con fuoco
pizz.
arco

tr
ff
sempre più f
f

f
sf
tr
f con fuoco
f con fuoco

sempre stacc.
p espress.

p
cresc.
mf
f
ff

Quintet No. 1 in A Major, Op. 18

p
p
p
p
p
p
p
pp
pp
pp
pp
cresc.
cresc.
cresc.
cresc.
cresc.
f
f
cresc.
cresc.
sf
sf
ff
sf
sf
f
f
cresc.
cresc.
ff
sf
sf
ff
sf
sf
f
cresc.
ff
sf
sf

sf
ff
f
p
ten.
espress.
pp
stacc.
pizz.

pizz.
arco
pp stacc.
pp
1.
2.
cresc.
f
dim.
p

stacc.
pp
pp
p
pp
stacc.
p
pp
p
pp
p
3
3
3
p
p
p
p
p cresc.
cresc.
cresc.
cresc.
cresc.
cresc.
cresc.
p
p
cresc.
cresc.
mf
mf
mf
cresc.
cresc.
cresc.
p
p
p
p
p
cresc.
cresc.
mf
cresc.
p

cresc.
con fuoco

ff
f
dim.
p
pp

tranquillo
p
cresc.
cresc.
cresc.
cresc.
pp
pp
stacc.
pp
stacc.
pp
stacc.
pizz.
pp
pp stacc.
pp stacc.
pp stacc.
cresc.
cresc.
cresc.
arco
cresc.
p
p
p
p
p
p
p
p
p
p

cresc.
p
sf
f
ten.

pp
pp stacc.
pp stacc.
pp stacc.
pizz.
pizz.
pizz.
arco
arco
pp
arco
pp
pp
espress.
cresc.
cresc.
cresc.
cresc.
espress.

cresc.
dim.
arco
f
p
sf

Intermezzo.

Andante sostenuto.

dim.
cre - scen - do

f
cresc.
ff
dim.
p
pp
f sempre
sf
p espress.
mf

pp
cresc.
sf
p
pp
dim.
espress.
f
sf
dim.

dolce
dim.
cresc.
più f

dim.
p
sf
f
dolce
pp
cre - scen - do
dim.

Scherzo.

Allegro di molto.

sempre stacc.
pp
pp
sempre stacc.
sempre stacc.

pp
pp
pp
pp
pp
pp espress.
pp
pp
espress.
pp
pp
sf
p
pp
pp
pp
pp
p
pizz.

arco
pp
p espress.
p
p
pp

pp
cresc.
f
ff
p
stacc.

tr
stacc.
p
pp
ff

p stacc.
p stacc.
p stacc.
cresc.
cresc.
cresc.

f
ff stacc.
ff stacc.
ff stacc.
dim.
p
p
pp
stacc.
pp
stacc.
p

cresc.
dim.
f
p
pp
trem.
stacc.
pizz.

Allegro vivace.
mf
p
cresc.
f
ff
sf
tr

pizz.
arco
espress.
cresc.
dim.
f
ff
sf
p

cresc.
cresc.
cresc.
cresc.
cresc.
cresc.
cresc.
cresc.
cresc.
f
f
f
f
f
cresc.
cresc.
cresc.
cresc.
cresc.
ff stacc.
ff stacc.
ff stacc.
ff stacc.
ff stacc.
f
cresc.
sf
p
ff
sempre
ff
sempre
ff
sempre
ff
sempre
ff
sempre
ff
sf
sf
sf
sf
p
pp
sfp
dim.
pp

cresc.
dim.
p
f
f sempre

cresc.
sf cresc. sf
sf cresc. sf
sf cresc. sf

con forza
stacc.
con forza
con forza
con forza
con forza

non ligato
con forza
nonligato
nonligato
nonligato
nonligato

dim.
dim.
dim.
dim.
dim.
poco a poco
poco a poco
poco a poco
poco a poco
poco a poco
non ligato
non ligato

cresc.
f
sf
ff
fp
p

p
cresc.
ff
sf
f
ff

Quintet No. 2 in B-flat Major, Op. 87

cresc.
p cresc.
cresc.
p cresc.
p cresc.
sf
ff
sfp
p
ff sf

p
sf
p
p
p
p
p
sf
sf
sf
dim.
cresc.
pizz.
arco
f

sf
f
ff
fp
p
cresc.
più f

ff
sf
dim.
p
pp
p dim.
cresc.
f

cresc.
f
p cresc.
p
cresc.
p
sf
sempre f
sf sempre f

dim.
cresc.

cresc.

dim.
cresc.
pizz.
arco
cresc

sf
ff
fp
p
cresc.
f
più f

dim.
sf
p
pp
cresc.
dimin.
f

cresc.
f
ff
sf

Andante scherzando.
pizz.
arco
cresc.
tr
sf

p
tr
cresc.
dim.
pizz.
arco
p tr
dim.
cresc.
pizz.
cresc.
dim.

pp
pizz.
arco
cresc.
f
sf
p
tr
dim.

cresc.
dim.
p
pizz.
arco
sf
f
pp
fsf

Adagio e lento.
pp
sf
p
cresc.
f
dim.
stacc.
sf con forza
fsf

p
cresc.
fp
cresc.
f
dim.
p dolce
sf
pp
ftrem.
ftrem.
sf

cresc.
f trem.
sf
p
dim.
f sf
sempre dim.
pp
pp sempre

p
dim.
pp
cresc.
f
fp
dim.

trem.
trem.
cresc.
sempre f
dim.
tranquillo
attacca

Allegro molto vivace.

cresc.
f
sf p
p
sf
dim.
sempre dim.
pp
cresc.
sf

cresc.
cresc.
cresc.
cresc.
cresc.
sempre f

sempre f
sempre f
sempre f
sempre f
sempre f

con fuoco
cresc.
ff
fp
p
f

p
cresc.
p
sf p
cresc.
p
sf p
cresc.
p
sf p
cresc.
p
sf p
cresc.
p
p
cresc.
sf p
cresc.
cresc.
f
sf p
cresc.
cresc.
f
p
f
p
cresc.
f
sf
dim.
sempre dim.
pp
dim.
sempre dim.
pp
dim.
sempre dim.
pp
pp
dim.
sempre dim.
pp
p dim.
sempre dim.
pp
cresc.
cresc.
cresc.
cresc.
cresc.

f
cresc.
sf
ff
sempre ff

Quartet No. 1 in E-flat Major, Op. 12

cresc.
al
dim.
dolce
a tempo
fritard.
espress.
ri_tar_dan_do

a tempo
cresc.
dim.
a tempo
cresc.
al

cresc.
ff espress.
espress.
dim.
pp sempre
ritard.
poco a poco
a tempo
dolce
ritard.
a tempo

cresc.
dim.
tranquillo

dolce
sfp
pp
sf
p
dim.
cresc.
sf p
pp
al
f
espress.

Canzonetta.

pp
stacc.
sempre pp
1.
2.
pizz.
arco
p

arco
pizz.
a tempo
ritard.
Andante espressivo.
largo
cresc.
dim.

con fuoco
cresc.
sempre
cresc.
al
espress.
tranquillo
largo
dim.
ten.
cresc. al
ff con fuoco
con fuoco
dim.
p espress.
espress.

cresc.
al
ff espress.
p tranquillo
dim.
p dim.
dolce
espress.
pp
attacca
Molto allegro e vivace.

dim.
cresc.
al
p con fuoco
pp

pp
cresc.
f
sf
ff
p
dim.
dol. tranquillo
tranquillo
ten.

al - - sf - -
f
sf
sf
sf
dim. - al -
p
cresc.
ff
ff con fuoco
ff con fuoco
ff con fuoco
ff con fuoco
ff
sf
fff

L'istesso tempo.
dim.
espress.
L'istesso tempo.
cresc.
dim.

dim.
cresc.

con fuoco
p cresc.
cresc.
dim.
p agitato
cresc.
p espress.
pp

cresc.
sf
p
pizz.
f
cresc. - al -
arco
ff

L'istesso tempo.
espress.
sempre f
dim.
espress.
ad lib.
a tempo
dim. pp
cresc.
dolce

dolce
dolce
dolce
p
p
p
cresc.
cresc.
p cresc.
cresc.
al
al
al
al
f
f
f
f
cresc.
cresc.
cresc.
f
f
f
dol. espress.
dim.
dim.
dim.
dim.
p dim.
p dim.
p dim.
pp
pp
pp
pp
p
p
p
p
dim.
dim.
dim.
dim.
pp
pp
pp
espress.
cresc.
cresc.
cresc.
dim.
dim.
dim.
cresc.
dim.
p
p
p
pp
pp
pp
pp
pp
pp
pp

THEMA.

Con moto.
Singstimme.
Pianoforte.
Ist es wahr? ist es wahr? dass du stets dort in dem
Laubgang, an der Wein-wand mei-ner harrst und den Mondschein und die Stern-lein auch nach
mir be-fragst? Ist es wahr? Sprich! Was ich fühle, das be-greift nur, die es
mitfühlt, und die treu mir e-wig, treu mir e-wig, e - wig bleibt.
(Voss.)

Quartet No. 2 in A Major, Op. 13

espress.
dim.
cresc.
agitato

cresc.
con fuoco
agitato
dim.
cresc.
dim.
cresc.

f
ff
pp
p
cresc.
poco a poco
al
sf
dim.
pizz.

dim.
pp poco ritard.
espress.
a tempo
poco ritard.
arco
pp poco ritard.
cresc.
al
cresc.
dim.
espress.

espress.
pizz.
arco
pizz.
arco
espress.
cresc.
con fuoco
cresc.
al
cresc.
al

dim.
p
pp
con fuoco
cresc.
poco
a
poco
sf
sempre cresc.
espress.
f
ff

con fuoco
cresc.
al
espress.
Adagio non lento.
cantabile
dim.

espress.
cresc.
sf
poco più animato.
dim.
poco ritard.
pizz.
sempre p
arco

arco
cresc.
più f
cresc. marcato
sempre più f
sempre f
pizz.
f arco
al
espress.
ff espress.

ad lib.
dim.
ritard.
Tempo I.
cresc.
espress.
ligato
dolce
espressivo
pp ligato

Intermezzo.

Allegretto con moto.

pp
pp
pp
p
p
p
pp
p
p
espress.
pp espress.
pp
p
pp
pp
stacc.
pp
stacc.
pp

stacc.
1.
2.
pizz.
ritard.
sempre ritard.
al
Tempo I.
arco
espress.
pp
p

poco accelerando
pizz.
arco poco accelerando
arco
poco accelerando
dim.
Presto.
ad libitum
a tempo
trem.
tempo

cresc.
dim.
pp
espress.
pizz.
arco
sf

arco
cresc.
mf
stacc.
ad libitum dim.

p
espress.
espress.
p espress.
pp
cresc.
f
ff
sf
tr
f non ligato

p
cresc.
f
cresc.
p
cresc.
f
f>
cresc.
ff non ligato
ff non ligato
ff non ligato
ff non ligato
p
p
pp
p
p
dim.
f espress.
f dim.
p
p
p
p

cresc.
dim.
simili
non ligato

dim.
espress.
cresc.
al

dim.
cresc.
non ligato
non ligato
cresc.
cresc.
ff non ligato
ff non ligato
ff non ligato

dim.
pp
p
espress.
f
a piacere quasi una fantasia
dim. e ritard.
ritard.
Adagio non lento.
Recit.
Adagio come I.
cresc.
mf
dolce
f cantando
con moto
cantando
cresc. - al -
dim. - al

Quartet No. 3 in D Major, Op. 44, No. 1

Molto Allegro vivace. M.M. $\frac{d}{}$=88.

ff
fp
tr
mf
sfp
f
dimin.
p
dolce
cresc.
sf
pp
sempre pp

cresc.
pizz.
arco
cre
scen
do al
più
con fuoco
tr

tr
f
sf
p
cresc.
fp
cre
scen
do
scendo

leggiero
tr
sempre p
pizz.
sempre pp
cresc.
dimin.
leggiero
leggiero
arco
sempre cresc.

f
dimin.
sf
mf
sempre dimin.
pp
pp poco
a
cresc.
poco
al
ff
fp
tr
p

cresc.
pizz.
arco

cresc.
cre
scen
do
sempre f
più f
con fuoco
ff

cresc.
cresc.
cresc.
cresc.
cresc.
cresc.
cresc.
cresc.
al
al
al
al

MENUETTO.

Un poco Allegretto. M.M. 𝅗𝅥. = 60.

1.
2.
espressivo
p
pp
cresc.
f
sf
dim.

cresc.
dim.
pizz.
arco
pp
p
f
sf

cresc.
dim.
Andante espressivo ma con moto. M.M. ♪= 126.
pizz.
pizz.
arco
cresc.

cresc.
arco
dim.
cantabile
p
f
sf

cresc.
al
p
f
sf
più f
dim.
pizz.
tr
arco
pp
cantabile

cresc.
dim.
pizz.
arco
tr
al
leggiero

a tempo
tr
sf
marc.
f
dim.
ritard.
p
a tempo
cresc.
pizz.
pp
Presto con brio. M.M. 𝅗𝅥. = 104.

sf
p
dimin.
pp
cresc.
f
cre - scen - do - al -
più f
mf
sfp

cantabile
cresc.
sf cresc.
cresc.
sf cresc.
cresc. -

cresc.
più f
cresc.

sf
cresc.
p
f
dimin.

cresc.
dimin.
cantabile
pizz.
marcato
p cresc.
arco
marcato

cresc.
marcato
cresc.
f
sf
sf più f
più f
ff
p
ff

dimin.
dimin.
dimin.
cresc.
cresc.
cresc.
cresc.
cresc.
cresc.
cresc.

cresc.
cresc.
cresc.
cresc.
sf marcato
ff marcato
marcato
f marcato
f marcato
fp

cresc.
f
ff
sf
p
cre - scen - do
cresc.

Quartet No. 4 in E Minor, Op. 44, No. 2

Allegro assai appasionato. M.M. 𝅗𝅥=88.

cresc.
cresc.
dimin.

dimin.
pp
p
cresc.
sf
f
ff con fuoco
dimin.

dimin.
sf
p
pp
cresc.
f
cre
scen
do
sempre cresc.
al

cresc.
sf
cre
al
scen
do
f
più f

ff
dimin.
p
pp
pizz.
arco
sempre p
cresc.
sf

cresc.
dimin.
dolce

cresc.
ff con fuoco
dimin.
cre - scen - do

ff
sf
f
p
tranquillo
pp
cresc.
cre - scen - do

SCHERZO.

Allegro di molto. ♩. = 72.

cresc.
cresc.
cresc.
cresc.
cre scen do al
molto cresc. al
molto cresc. al

cresc.
dimin.
sempre dimin.
pizz.

pp
arco
cresc.
f
p
staccato
sf
dimin.

dimin.
pizz.
dolce
arco
pizz.

 NB. Dieses Stück darf durchaus nicht schleppend gespielt werden.*

Andante. ♩=60.

* This movement must by no means be dragged.

cresc.
cre - - scen - - do
cresc.
dimin.
p espress.
dimin.

cresc.
cresc.
cresc.
cresc.
cresc.
cresc.
dimin.
dimin.
dimin.
dimin.
dimin.
dimin.
dolce
dimin.
dimin.
dimin.
cresc.
cresc.
cresc.
cresc.
cresc.
cresc.
cresc.
cresc.
cresc.
cresc.
cresc.
cresc.

cresc.
dimin.
espress.
cresc.
dimin.

Presto agitato. 𝅗𝅥. = 72.

cresc.
cresc.
cresc.
cresc.
cresc.
cresc.
cresc.
cresc.
cresc.
cresc.
cresc.
cresc.

Animato.
cresc.
p leggiero
pizz.

tr
arco
dimin.
cresc.
cre - scen
do - al

p staccato
staccato
cresc.
pizz.

cresc.
arco
cre

cre - scen - do
dimi - nuen - do
dimin.
cresc.
dimin.
cresc.

cresc.
p leggiero

tr
p con fuoco
pizz.
arco
cresc.
dimin.

cresc.
cresc.
cresc.
cresc.
cresc.
dimin.
cresc.
cresc.
cresc.
cresc. poco a poco
sempre cresc.
più f
più f
più f
più f
al

Quartet No. 5 in E-flat Major, Op. 44, No. 3

cresc.
sempre p

cresc.
sf
p
f
dim.
pp
mf

p dolce
cresc.
stacc.
dim.

cresc.
più f
ff
al
sf
p dolce

p
dim.
dol.
pp
poco a
poco a poco cresc.
poco cresc.
cresc. poco a poco
al
cresc.
f
ff
mf
sf

cresc.
ff
f
p
cresc.
sf
fp
sempre

cresc.
al
dim.
mf
pp
f
p
sf

arco
pizz.
p
pp
dim.
cresc.
sf
f
al
f con forza

ff
sf
dim.
pizz.
arco
pp
cresc.
più f

SCHERZO.

Assai leggiero vivace. ♩. = 152.

cresc.
dim.
stacc.
leggiero

cresc.
dim.
espress.
stacc.

ritard. poco a poco
a tempo
ritard. poco a poco
a tempo
ritard. poco a poco
a tempo
ritard. poco a poco
a tempo
cresc.
al
ff

tr
sf
ff
p
stacc.
cresc.
f
al
fp

pp
sf
p
dim.
f
molto cresc.
pizz.

Adagio non troppo. ♩= 54.

cresc.
f
dim.
cresc.
dim.
cresc.
dim.
cresc.
f
dim.
pp
pp
pp
pp
tr
pp
tr
cresc.
cresc.
cresc.
f
f
f
sf
sf
cresc.
dim.
dim.
pp espressivo
pp
sf
pp espressivo
sf
espress.
p
sf
cresc.
cresc.
cresc.
p espress.
cresc.
sf
sf
sempre cresc.
sf
sempre cresc.
sf
sempre cresc.
sf
f
f
f
f
sf
sf

ff
dim.
pp
espress.
sf
p
cresc.
f

cresc.
cresc.
dim.
dim.
dim.
espress.
espressivo
cresc.
dim.
dim.
dim.

Molto Allegro con fuoco. 𝅗𝅥 = 76.

cresc.
cresc.
cresc.
cresc.
cresc.
stacc.
stacc.
stacc.
cantabile
stacc.

sf
dim.
p
tr
pp
cresc.
f

ff
ff
ff
ff
p
sf
p
p
p
sf
dim.
dim.
dim.
dim.
dim.
dim.
dim.
pp
pp
pp
pp
pp
pizz.
espress.
pizz.
arco
pp
pp
p
p
cresc.
cresc.
pizz.

cresc.
arco
dim.

cresc.
sempre cresc.

cresc.
dim.
più

cresc.
dim.
sempre f

stacc.
cantabile
dim.
p dol.
pp
cresc.

cresc.
cresc.
cresc.
cresc.

Quartet No. 6 in F Minor, Op. 80

cresc.

p cresc.
cresc.
dim.
pp
fp
sf
f cresc.
f

p
pp
sempre p
pp
sempre p
pp
sempre p
pp
cresc.
poco
a
poco
f
f
f
f
f
sf
ff sf
sf
f
sf
più f
sf
sf
sf
sf
sf
sf
sf
f
sempre più f
ff
ff
sf
ff
ff
fp
ff
ff
sf
sempre più f
fp
p
sf
sf
sf
sf
cresc.
ff
ff
ff

cresc.
dim.

sf
sf
cresc.
cresc.
cresc.
cresc.
p
p
p
p
cresc.
pp cresc.
cresc.
pp cresc.
cresc.
pp cresc.
cresc.
pp cresc.
cresc.
cresc.
cresc.
p
pp cresc.
cresc.
p
p
pp cresc.
cresc.
p
p
pp cresc.
cresc.
p
p
pp cresc.
cresc.
p
p
dim.
pp
fp
dim.
pp
fp
dim.
pp
fp
dim.
pp
fp

fp
cresc.
f
sf
con forza
sempre più
ff
accele - ran - do poco a poco
sino - al
Presto.

Allegro assai.

fsf
sf
ff
sf
p
cresc.
f
cresc.
ff
p
pizz.
pp
1. arco
f
2.
arco
p
arco
p

p
cresc.
sf
dim.
f
ff

cresc.

pizz.
arco
pp
p
cresc.
dim.
Adagio.
sf
f

cresc.
p
f
pp
dim.
sf

cresc.
sempre cresc.
ff
sf
al
dim.
pp
cantabile

Finale.

Allegro molto.

cresc.
dim.
cresc.
dim.
cresc.
cresc.
cresc.

cresc.
dim.
sempre dim.

cresc.
dim.

pp
sempre pp
pizz.
arco
cresc.
ff
p

cresc.
dim.

p
cresc.
cresc.
p
cresc.
cresc.
cresc.
cresc.
cresc.
cresc.
f
f
f
f
più f
più f
più f
più f
sf
sf
sf
sf
con fuoco
ff
ff
ff
ff
sempre ff
sempre ff
sempre ff
sempre ff
ff
ff
ff
ff
sf
sf
sf
sf

sempre ff
sempre ff
sempre ff
sempre ff

Four Pieces for String Quartet, Op. 81

TEMA CON VARIAZIONI.

Andante sostenuto.

Un poco più animato.
cresc.
dim.
arco
sf
f
p

cresc.
cresc.
cresc.
cresc.
mf
mf
mf
mf
dim.
dim.
p
p
p
p
cresc.
cresc.
cresc.
cresc.
f
f
f
f
p
p
p
p
cresc.
cresc.
cresc.
cresc.
cresc.
cresc.
cresc.
f
f
f
f
più f
ff
ff
ff

Presto.

Andante come I.
ritard.
cresc.
dim.
al
pizz.
arco

SCHERZO.

pizz.
pizz.
arco
arco
arco
pizz.
arco
arco

cresc.
ff
p
tr
pizz.

cresc.
arco
dim.

tr
cresc.
f
p
pizz.
pizz.
p
p
cresc.
f
cresc.
f

CAPRICCIO.

Andante con moto.

dim.
pp
cresc.
f
arco
pp cresc.
p
cresc.
sf
dim.
pizz.
fp
Allegro fugato, assai vivace.

f
p
cresc.
fp
sf
pizz.
arco

cresc.
pizz.
arco
più f

fp
p
cresc.
f
sf
più f
ff

ff
ff
ff
ff
p
cresc.
fp
cresc.
fp
cresc.
fp
cresc.
sf
f
sf
più f
f
sf
sf
più f
f
sf
sf
f
più f
sf
sf
sf
sf
sf più f
sf
sf
sf
ff
ff
ff
ff
sf
sf
sf
ff con fuoco
dim.
p
p
p
pizz.
p
cresc.
cresc.
cresc.
cresc.
cresc.
cresc.
arco
cresc.
cresc.
f
sf
f
sf
f
sf
f
sf

sf
p
pizz.
cresc.
arco
f
fp
ff

FUGA.

A tempo ordinario. (M. M. 𝅗𝅥 = 104.)

p
pp
pp
pp
pp
pp
p

cresc.
dim.
con espress.
dol.